Contents

Penguin

Penguins are flightless birds that spend half of their time in the sea. Most can be found in the **southern hemisphere**. They use their wings like flippers to power their way through the water. They feed on fish and squid, catching them in their beaks underwater.

Inside Animals

Birds

David West

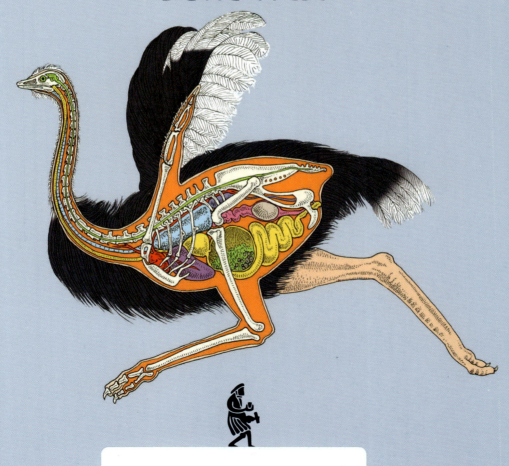

Wayland
First published in Great Britain in 2018 by Hodder and Stoughton

Designed and illustrated by David West

HB ISBN 978 1 5263 1083 5
PB ISBN 978 1 5263 1084 2

Printed in Malaysia

Wayland
An imprint of
Hachette Children's Group
Carmelite House
50 Victoria Embankment
London EC4Y 0DZ

An Hachette UK Company
www.hachette.co.uk

www.wayland.co.uk

INSIDE ANIMALS BIRDS
was produced for Wayland by
David West Children's Books, 11 Glebe Road, London SW13 0DR

This king penguin dives to depths of more than 100 metres and has been known to go as deep as 300 metres when chasing its prey.

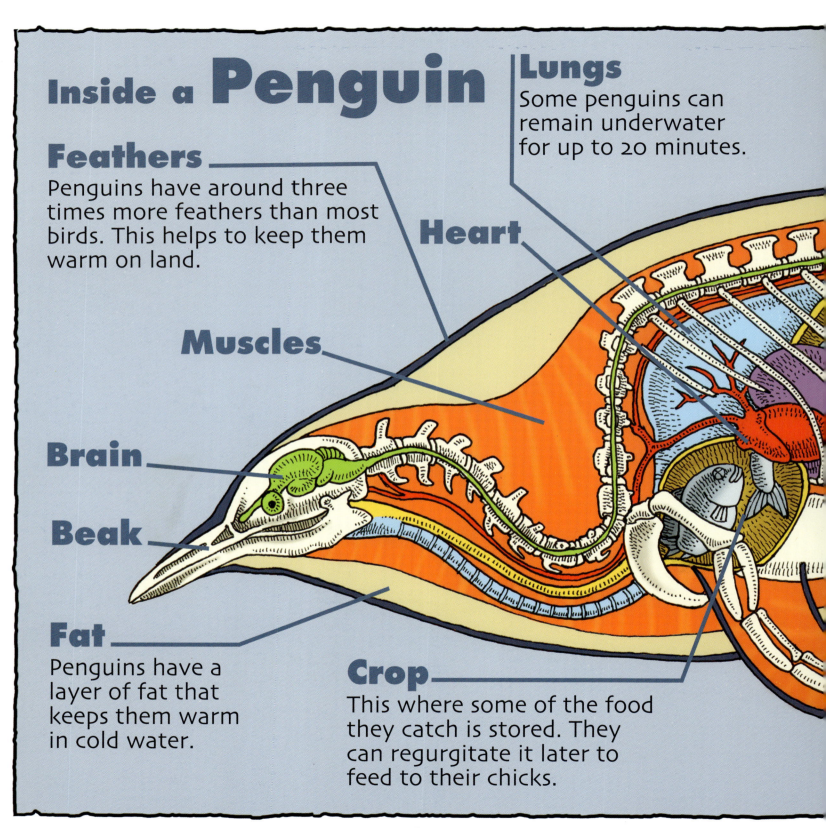

Inside a **Penguin**

Lungs
Some penguins can remain underwater for up to 20 minutes.

Feathers
Penguins have around three times more feathers than most birds. This helps to keep them warm on land.

Heart

Muscles

Brain

Beak

Fat
Penguins have a layer of fat that keeps them warm in cold water.

Crop
This where some of the food they catch is stored. They can regurgitate it later to feed to their chicks.

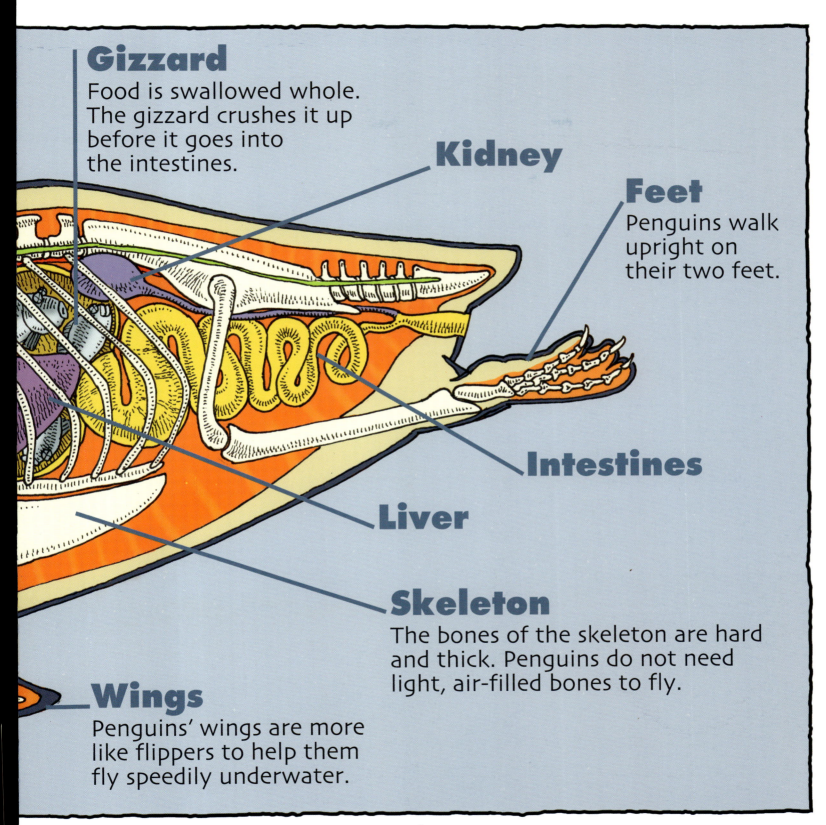

Gizzard

Food is swallowed whole. The gizzard crushes it up before it goes into the intestines.

Kidney

Feet

Penguins walk upright on their two feet.

Intestines

Liver

Skeleton

The bones of the skeleton are hard and thick. Penguins do not need light, air-filled bones to fly.

Wings

Penguins' wings are more like flippers to help them fly speedily underwater.

Chicken

Chickens are birds that are farmed for their eggs and as food. Females are called hens and males are called cockerels or roosters. They eat seeds and insects which they find by scratching the ground. In the wild they may even eat small animals like lizards and mice. Chickens live together in flocks. They have a social order where some have first rights to food. This is known as a 'pecking order'.

*Chickens are descended from the red junglefowl and can fly a short distance. Usually it is to **roost** in a tree or to escape a **predator**, otherwise they don't bother.*

9

Inside a **Chicken**

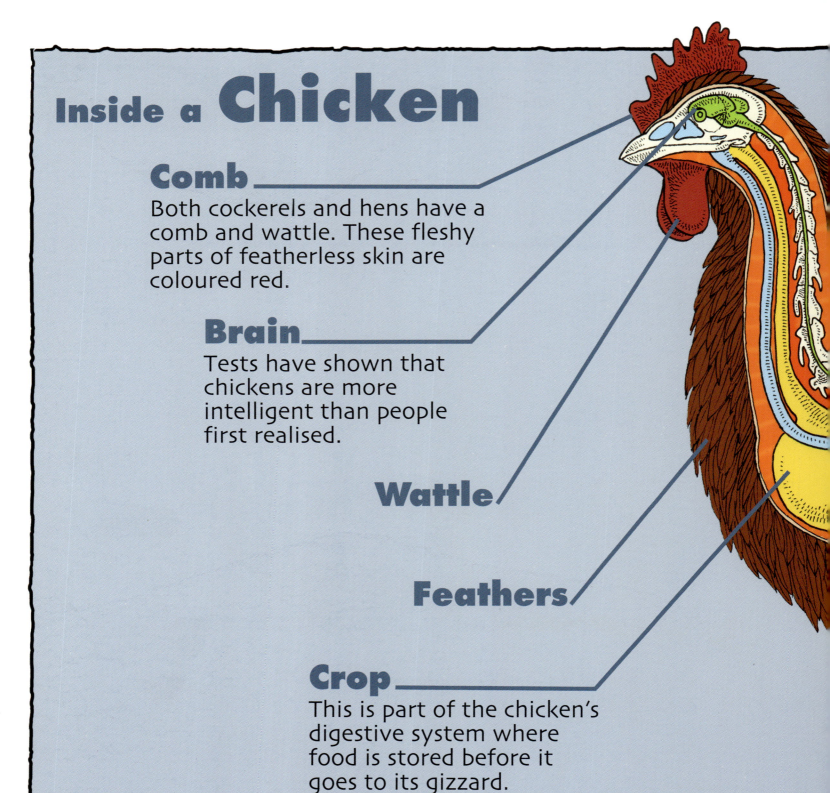

Comb
Both cockerels and hens have a comb and wattle. These fleshy parts of featherless skin are coloured red.

Brain
Tests have shown that chickens are more intelligent than people first realised.

Wattle

Feathers

Crop
This is part of the chicken's digestive system where food is stored before it goes to its gizzard.

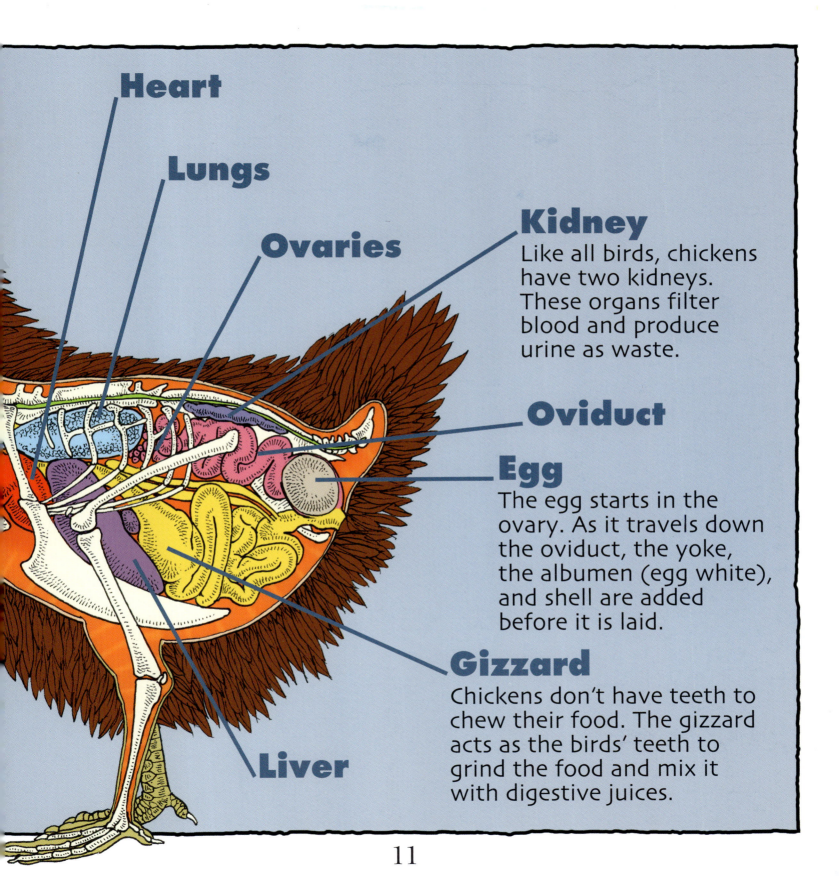

Heart

Lungs

Ovaries

Kidney
Like all birds, chickens have two kidneys. These organs filter blood and produce urine as waste.

Oviduct

Egg
The egg starts in the ovary. As it travels down the oviduct, the yoke, the albumen (egg white), and shell are added before it is laid.

Gizzard
Chickens don't have teeth to chew their food. The gizzard acts as the birds' teeth to grind the food and mix it with digestive juices.

Liver

Owl

Owls are **birds of prey** that hunt at night. They have very good night vision and can rotate their heads and necks as much as 270°. They use their special ears to detect prey at night. They hunt insects, birds and small mammals such as mice.

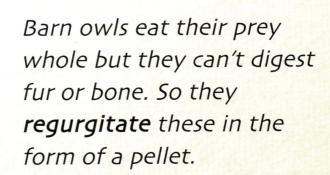

Barn owls eat their prey whole but they can't digest fur or bone. So they **regurgitate** these in the form of a pellet.

Inside an Owl

Brain

Eyes

Barn owls' eyes are twice as good as human eyes in the dark. They can see movement at night.

Face

Barn owls have a flat, disc-shaped face that collects and directs sound towards the ears.

Beak

Like other birds of prey barn owls have sharp, hooked beaks which they use to tear up their food.

Ears

Barn owls have the best hearing of all animals. They can capture prey in total darkness by hearing alone.

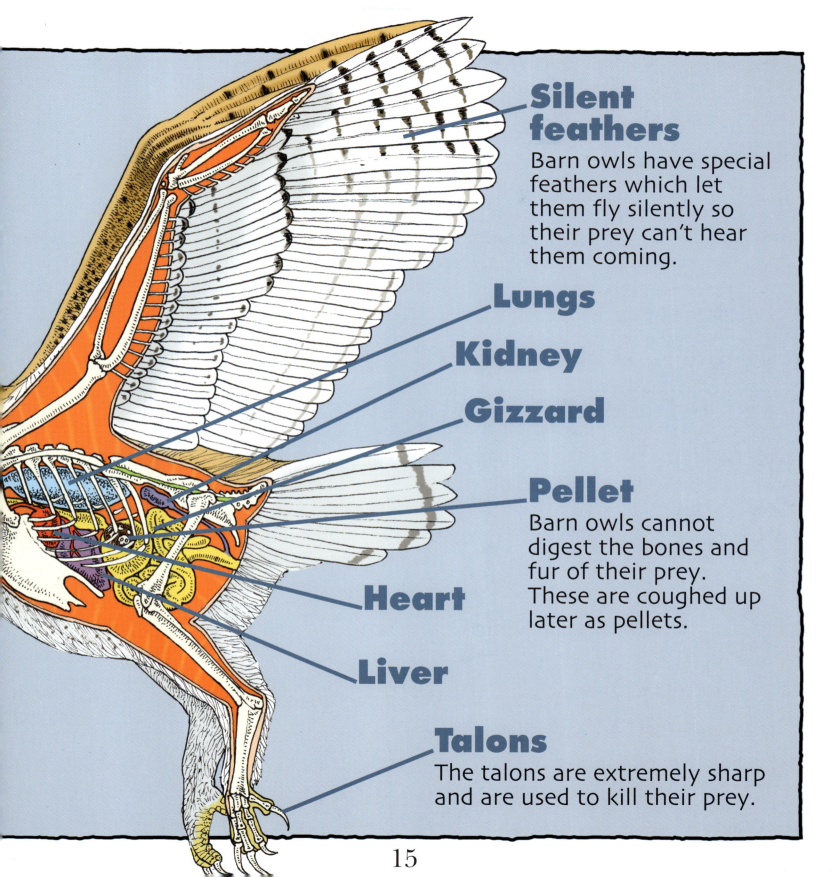

Silent feathers

Barn owls have special feathers which let them fly silently so their prey can't hear them coming.

Lungs

Kidney

Gizzard

Pellet

Barn owls cannot digest the bones and fur of their prey. These are coughed up later as pellets.

Heart

Liver

Talons

The talons are extremely sharp and are used to kill their prey.

Parrot

Parrots are intelligent birds that can **mimic** human speech. They are often kept as pets for their beautiful colouring. In the wild they spend much of their time climbing around tree canopies. They also use their beak for climbing by gripping branches with it. They feed mainly on nuts, seeds and fruits.

This parrot is called a love bird because it pairs up with a partner for life. Pairs spend a lot of time perched on branches next to each other. They are among the smallest parrots and live in Africa and Madagascar.

Inside a **Parrot**

Skeleton

A bird's skeleton is extremely light and strong. The bones are filled with holes.

Brain

Parrots are intelligent. They have more brain cells than apes, despite having much smaller brains.

Beak

Parrots use their sharp beaks to defend themselves. They also use them to crack nuts and peel fruits.

Air sacs

Birds need to breathe lots of air to get enough oxygen for their muscles to fly. As well as lungs they have up to eight air sacs around the body.

Crop

Keel

This breast bone is where the large flying muscles are attached.

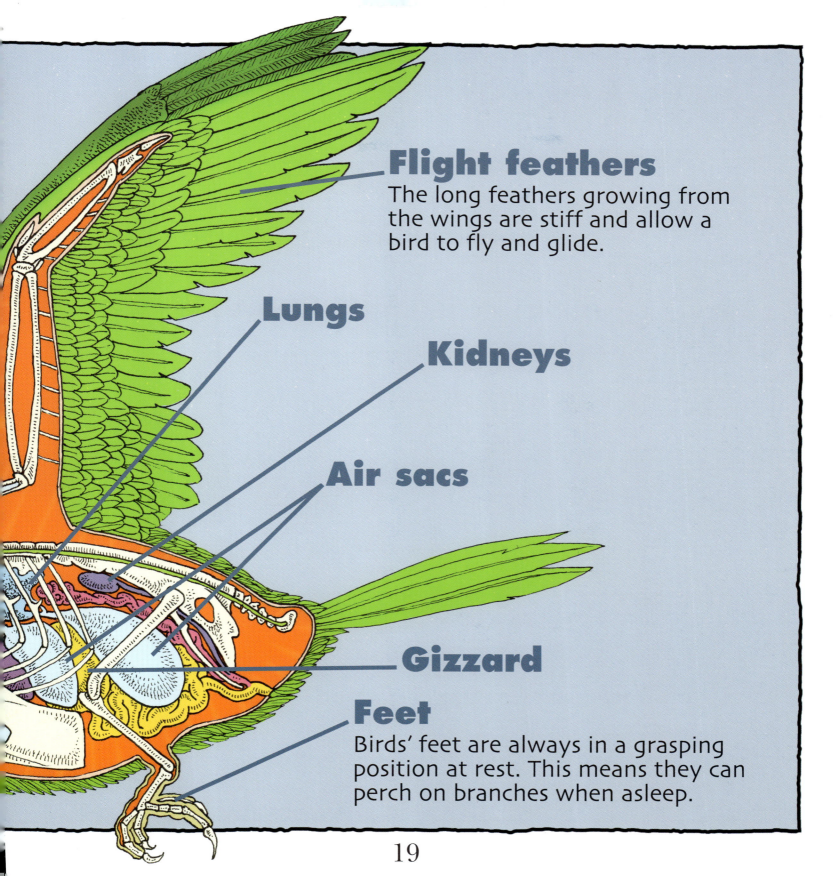

Flight feathers
The long feathers growing from
the wings are stiff and allow a
bird to fly and glide.

Lungs

Kidneys

Air sacs

Gizzard

Feet
Birds' feet are always in a grasping
position at rest. This means they can
perch on branches when asleep.

Ostrich

The ostrich is a flightless bird. It is also the largest living bird. Ostriches are fast runners and can sprint at more than 70 kph (43.5 mph), covering up to five metres in a single stride. Their strong legs are used in self defence against predators. Their kick is so powerful it can kill a lion. Ostriches live in wandering groups of between five to fifty birds.

When threatened an ostrich will lie flat on the ground or run away. Sometimes it might kick out to defend itself. But it never hides its head in the sand.

Inside an **Ostrich**

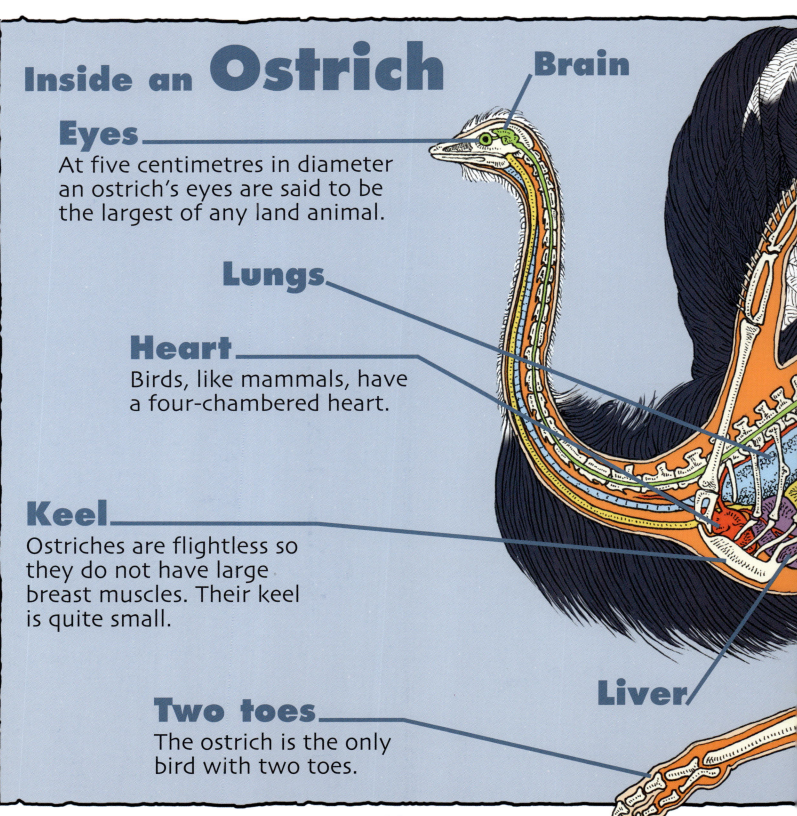

Brain

Eyes

At five centimetres in diameter an ostrich's eyes are said to be the largest of any land animal.

Lungs

Heart

Birds, like mammals, have a four-chambered heart.

Keel

Ostriches are flightless so they do not have large breast muscles. Their keel is quite small.

Liver

Two toes

The ostrich is the only bird with two toes.

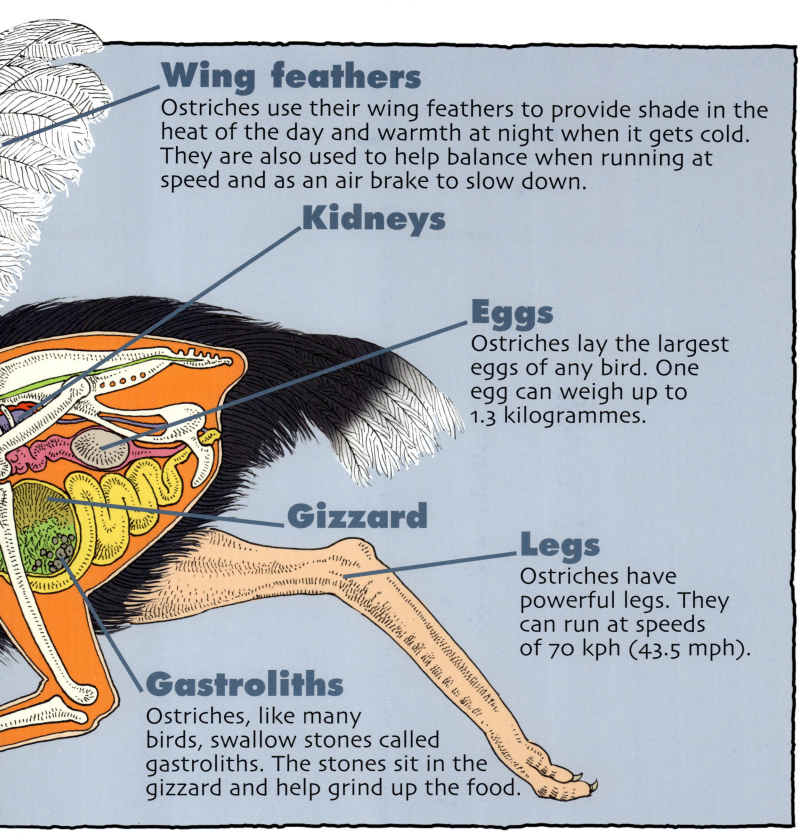

Wing feathers

Ostriches use their wing feathers to provide shade in the heat of the day and warmth at night when it gets cold. They are also used to help balance when running at speed and as an air brake to slow down.

Kidneys

Eggs

Ostriches lay the largest eggs of any bird. One egg can weigh up to 1.3 kilogrammes.

Gizzard

Legs

Ostriches have powerful legs. They can run at speeds of 70 kph (43.5 mph).

Gastroliths

Ostriches, like many birds, swallow stones called gastroliths. The stones sit in the gizzard and help grind up the food.

Glossary

birds of prey Also called raptors, these types of birds hunt other birds and small animals like rodents. They have powerful talons and curved, sharp beaks.
mimic Copy or imitate.
predator An animal that hunts and eats other animals.

regurgitate Bring swallowed food back up to the mouth.
roost A perch, such as a branch, on which birds rest at night.
southern hemisphere The half of planet Earth which is south of the equator.

Index